T0195557

A Heap of Living

KAITLIN GIBBS

authorHOUSE

AuthorHouse™
1663 Liberty Drive
Bloomington, IN 47403
www.authorhouse.com
Phone: 1 (800) 839-8640

Published by AuthorHouse 02/21/2020

ISBN: 978-1-7283-4794-3 (sc)
ISBN: 978-1-7283-4793-6 (e)

Print information available on the last page.

This book is printed on acid-free paper.

Contents

Dear Reader,

What constitutes a life well-lived? Most would get into a colloquy about existential moments, the measure of sheer felicity, the experiences, the company kept, etc. The answer, like the preponderance of existential questions, is within those who ask. There is no plausible way to configure a summation of how well a life was lived by simply denoting the subjective moments in your life. That is, if you live enough to reflect upon it.

The blatant truth is that I cannot simply speak on the life lived by another human; I can only provide a resource to which offers a perspective.

This book is an outlet of pain and truth of my life, so far, in my sententious years I have lived on this earth. At whatever stage in life you consider yourself to be in at this very moment, I hope this collection of poems offers you a certain gratitude that far expands cognitive comprehension. And I hope your soul finds peace with itself because God only knows the true semblance in that.

Hurticulture

I,
Myself,
Am a delicate flower:
My petals weathered
With every breath I take.
My whole heart is derived
From the acidulous touch
Of the fingertips of those
Who did not take my fragility
Into thought.

The Man Who Sold the World

As humans,
We're naturally inclined to hypocrisy;
Constantly denying
Our relentless existence
While we boast about
Some cheap piece we keep selling
To the famished people
We just-so-happen to stumble upon.
We are an all-but-justified species:
Constantly shifting to conform
To some arbitrary standard
Some wise man tried to substantiate
To make someone's life
Just as hapless as his.
The influencers of our lives
Are nothing more than a specter
Of our own humanities;
Telling us,
Screaming in our faces,
The verity to this whole life
We call ours,
While we drown out the pain
With anesthetics
Sold by the same wise guy
Who tried to sell you the secret to life.
But we stayed numb,
Trying to forget the consequences
Of trying to not feel a damn thing.

My Mother's Anguish

Glaring through the glass pane
Spitting out the rhymes of my years lived
Without you.
Your appearance:
Daunting and new
To represent the transition
Your incarceration led you to.
Black telephone presses
Up against my cheek and ear
Tears flowing in solitude
To match the steady flow of yours.
You say all is forgiven in your mind
And I believe you,
Truly,
For I remember the ache you transcribed
In the poetry of your first love-
The man that wrecked your soul and body
So much you felt fruitless.

Am I supposed to love you still?
When you tell me I'm pretty
And scrawny in the same sentence?
When you tell me you're sorry
After you left me
In a house of no remorse
or electricity;
With a shell of a father
That was destitute at the thought of you,

Who impoverished your body
Like the that of your first love?
I can't blame you for running,
For desiring a new life,
For crying and weeping internally.
I know not of the pain you endured
Through the trajectory of your life.
I can only remember you
As the mother I needed
During times I wish I felt your kiss,
Your embrace,
Your curly hair between my fingertips
One last time.
The bliss I felt at the sight of my own blood
The numbness I now feel at the thought
I had once understood.
You are my mother,
But I can never accept you anymore
As a person.
You can only exist as an entity
That retired into anguish.

And now you're aching in a cell
That broke you in the same way
Your first love-
As well as my father-
Did.

Oculus of Optimism

Sometimes at night,
I debate the argument of
Half full or half empty.
I usually say half full-
But I often ponder
The significance of the ladder.
I often wonder how my existence compares
To that of another.
Maybe that's the point:
Maybe this debate exists to define themselves.
If you only have one, what must it say
Of society?
What must we think?

My Dear, Depression

My dear,
We meet again.
You shake my hand as we exchange empty glances.
I have you with me,
Yet I feel as if I'm alone;
Lost,
Even.
You,
Guiding me into a direction
I'm all too familiar with.
Yet it feels as if I'm alien to it;
Tucking the blueprints
Into the back of my mind,
As a way of an attempt
At forgetting.
With you by my side,
Our hands entwined,
I see you bring out a part of me
I always wish to overlook.
Your presence weakens me
To my very bones.
But then again,
You are just a hallucination:
A facade conjured in the mind.
Almost immortal,
You are;
As I've made you into a persona-

One I'm not too sure of.
But I know you're there,
Lurking amongst the shadows
Of thoughts
Too dark to bear.

Long Gone and Cold

I was searching
For warmth in October,
Ravaging amongst old skeletons
And bones of past lives;
Only to find the coldness
That yields itself in defense
Of savage hands
That know not of its inexorable past.
Yet they gave into that touch,
For they know all too well
The pain those fingertips have felt.

The yearning in those eyes,
That plead for something:
Something that,
Unfortunately,
Cannot be remedied
Among the stale exoskeletons
Of those I had longed for.

From the Eyes of a Pauper

Expensive cars and picket fences:
So this is the standard of life
We cherish so deeply:
One that receives instead of gives?
Why is our own instinct
To take
Instead of give?
Even when we've gotten
Everything we could ever dream of?

Society tells us,
Commands us,
To act as princes
And to forget our times as paupers.
Because once we acquired the taste
Of such pleasantries,
We must never remember
The unforgiving grounds
That made us.

Blood Against Booze

The accusation in my eyes
Matched the contempt
In yours.

A pair it was:
Just like the alcohol
To your liver.

A toxic mix it was:
Both scorning each other's existence
To dust.

The Might in the Light

We wait for the light to become us,
But darling,
We can't hold a candle to the
Iridescence
That the sun brings upon us
Each day.
There's no doubt for her,
She's just gleaming for all she is,
And we expect this of her-
We even grimace when she can't glow
Because of the beautiful clouds
That feel so misunderstood.

Darling,
Just because you can't see her
Or feel her,
Even,
Doesn't mean she isn't there.
And that's the whole point of it all:
To love and not expect a damn thing in return.
Not because it's right,
No,
Because it's how we survive.

Soul Purpose

And I feel this tenderness
In my chest
Like it is about to cave in on me.
And I wonder,
Truly wonder,
If it's the repercussion
Of your effect on me-
If it's from
The loudness and persistence
Of this heart beating
Like its sole purpose is for
You.

Solitude in Destruction

The calm after the storm,
I suppose,
Is to create some sort of peace,
Or solace upon the chaos
That had since died down:
A compensation for the wreckage imposed upon us.
I find it quite intrinsic;
Beautiful,
Even,
How the storm itself was composed
To remind us of how nature
Creates things so powerful
That us tortured souls are forced to recognize
She's the one in control.
Sometimes the reminder
Not so friendly.

I find myself lost in it all
(As I suppose I should be).

It's odd how most find calm
Amongst the aftermath
When I'm so comfortably still
In the midst.

Age of Prohibition

There's champagne in my very veins-
Only bare water to those quenched
On other's custom bourbon.
Only a novelty to those searching for a
Stronger, more pungent mix.
We're all full of our own poison-
Carefully brewed,
Day upon day.
I guess it must say something about each of us
Who know not of the poison we contain.
Some nights I'll admit I get drunk on my own liquor.
You must know I'm really drowning,
As intoxication is rare with my blood type.
And the hangover lasts for days.
For there's no remedy to outrun
The madness pumped into my heart.
All I can do is hope I find someone
Who considers me as a refreshment,
Not a last-ditch effort to provide their fix
On the fine wine they inevitably crave.

Unrequited Inquiry

Am I un-loveable?
Am I just an un-loveable soul?
Who am I?
Who am I to you?
To him?
To her?
I need to know.
I need this bidding and bleak truth
Spilled out like my love for everyone else;
Splattered over the lattice of my DNA
And pronounced at the scene of which
Dictates the utter pain I am living In.
To see myself in others' eyes,
To finally understand why I'm never chosen,
Why I'm never someone who is needed;
Instead someone who is conditional,
With unconditional love overflowing from
An empty source of which is all too familiar.

In terms of dismay and silence,
I need to find the voice-
The biding voice that is telling others to flee
At the detestable site of me.

A Slow Death

Familiarity kills you slowly:
It takes you in during daunting times,
It wraps you in comfort,
Slaps you with a case of mistaken identity,
And inflames the ego.
You can say it has nurtured you,
But far too much it has-
Far be it from me to tell you this,
When I'm aching at the joints
From trying to bide inside an identity
I no longer fit,
Inside a house that never accepted me,
Inside a body that was never able to contain
The contents of my aching and bursting soul
Struggling to return to its home again.

From the Shadows of a Lost Mind

I can't help you
Fight the monsters
That lie just beyond your eyelids.
And I can't help you cope
With the hurt that is consuming your body.
Because that's not my job:
My line of work doesn't consist
Of helping you fight yourself
Because you can no longer accept
The darkest parts of you,
Scrambling to escape
Out of this safe haven
You call your mind.

You can't look at the naked light
Without touches of darkness,
Just like you can't live your life
In pure serenity,
Neglecting the parts of you
You can't bear to claim.

Red-Eye to the Promise Land

And I wish I could supply you with a way to surrender
But there's no possible way for you
To ignore this contender.
I can fib and say that it's your fight
But I know how that ends:
You leave on that dreaded flight.
Away from all else,
Where you wish you could be.
I can take you away from all that pain
But I can't promise there won't be any rain.

Upon the years of which you forfeited
In that dream of all loneliness,
You took my hand to try and relieve
But you only found a world full of emptiness.
I could tell you I can help
But you'd only end up dying,
From the wounds of which you've created-
On the day you became sedated.

I Needed Myself First

And I wanted to cry for you.
As I yearned,
As I ached,
To know the toughness of your fingertips
Upon my rosy cheeks.
To know the security
Your arms provided in an embrace,
To know how you see me in those
Ember eyes-
Those sad eyes that couldn't hide from me.
Those tired arms that carried yourself
Into another persona-
Not even I recognized.

God,
How I wanted you
In every way imaginable.
But it could never exist
In any way
Other than metaphorical.

Patience

Patience:
An important piece of significance
In all our lives.
For some,
It's an easy pill to swallow;
Others,
They need a bottle of whiskey to wash
It down.
The agony of waiting
The ambiguity,
It's all incapsulated
Into one thing:
The idea of calmness
That should wash over
As you enter the inevitable realms
Of possibility.
I suppose trust must also be a factor,
Not only the trusting of the world
To intertwine its roots between your fingers
To guide you
Unforgivingly,
While you also trust yourself
To not get swallowed up
By the serenity
Of the waves of uncertainty
Nature provides.

We're all so reliant on it all:
The bed that hugs us at night,
For example.
We even complain
About the weather and traffic
For its unpredictability
While we risk it all,
Unknowingly,
Every sacred second

Patience is something we learn
And that's just the answer
Most attempt to fully understand
But only some
Are able to take the final step.
And that's ultimately to accept
That,
Without patience,
You will never know
The kindhearted
And gentile caress
Of trust.

Purgatory

Its nights like these
Where I feel my soul's place
Has been mistaken
For that of someone else's.
And it's such a horribly forlorn feeling to feel
When you're finally surrounded
By those you adore most.
But you still feel this gnawing,
Throbbing loneliness,
And craving of somewhere else;
Somewhere that exceeds all
Blank expectations
And false limitations,
And sets a new precedent.
For a mistaken identity is not
Something to toy with.
I'm painfully uncomfortable
In this position of someone else's;
As it's not in my repertoire
To fill the place of someone
Who is long gone,
And never returning.

Road Less Travelled

The speedy flash of a headlight,
The gentle blink of an eye,
The ominous push of a pedal.
There it was before her:
The excuse she had been longing for,
The destination she had planned;
Yet,
Evidently,
Had no intentions of arriving.
A drive down some idle road
Did not lead her
To the place she wanted.
Instead,
It led to a moment
Of untimely guilt and despair.
A moment she'd later
Long to take back.

Arms stretching
Through the quantum of time;
A moment she'd constantly fathom
To somehow redo.
But at the time,
She was preoccupied:
The sunset,
For example,
Had chosen to make its debut
Amongst the clouds of uncertainty.

The picturesque moment
That she was led to
Held no lies or false truths.
It was only under colors of
Amaranth and calypso orange
Where she found her true destination:
Raw and unfiltered.
It was not final,
Despite the oratory
Of an age-old tale
Being told
For the very last time.

Momma's Hand-me-downs

Love:
A fickle concept,
An enigma,
Really.
Full of dubiety
And obscurity;
Yet,
Making those inflicted
So affixed
Among themselves.
My love
Far exceeds my limitations,
Or so I have come to discover.

Not having the nurturement
I desired
Caused me to somehow
Have an overabundance
That I feel in my bones.
It will soon run out,
As my joints have been protesting;
Helplessly trying to beat the clock,
I find myself
Lost
In one's
Uniquely modified infatuation:
Always in a tizzy
About a boy-

My mother's original mistake,
So generously handed down to me.
But it all comes down
To the terrible,
Retched actuality
That I'm rambling,
Still inebriated on the irremediable notion
That I shall not fully
Delve into the definition
Of love
Until I exert that very infatuation
Unto myself.

Time Slows When Life Lulls to Grief

When it's 10:17 at night
And I'm left alone
With nothing but my thoughts;
Pounding in my skull,
Punching at the very frontal lobe
At the very site
That conjured itself
And scraping at the
Residual effects
Of a terribly sad sight
Sojourn and bleak in its very nature.
A slap across the face,
As I seem to not feel
What is expected of me.

My tears have gotten
Far too sparse
As the guilt creeps up
Ever-so-gently
And placed upon
The hungry palms of my conscience.

Irrevocably,
It is now 10:25
And I am still stuck on it,
In hopes that my vagueness
Doesn't lose its sick punch.

It is now too much to ask
Yet,
I will ask away.
Naively,
In my last gasp of air
Due to a long-drawn sigh.
Because curiosity may have killed the cat,
But the pain always wins
In mortal combat.

Hunger Pains

Another drop in the void.
Tell them about those
Agonizing times of which
You could not conjure up a tear.
But,
Oh,
How you should've.
Go on now.
Enlighten them!
With retrospect
And immortality,
Tell them how you've gone so long hungry
But the thought of a feast
Brings you to your very knees.
A letter to self;
You are reading.
Attempting to compensate
For past egos
Drowned in unforgiving pain
And dubious insecurity.

Lying Linguists

Many argue
Abstract art
Is not art
Simply by the judgement
Of its simplistic complexities.
That's because
It is only surface level evaluation;
They cannot possibly
Contemplate
The jagged lines
Or the forceful splotches.

Art is a language unspoken,
But to them,
Its gobbledygook,
Anyway,
Yelling in precocious sincerity.

The whole thing about it is that
Humanity tends to undercut
A masterpiece
Simply because
It's not something understood.

Cincture of Sanity

Take my hand.
Hold it tightly,
Desperately,
Wildly,
And hungrily.
I might sound desperate
But don't tread lightly.

I need you for the healing.
It's not just a feeling.
Engulf me;
In all gratitude
And innumerable measure
Of solicitude.
At least,
Before this feeling
Subsides to grief
Like the sun subsides
To land:
Think of me
However you may.
And remember me
Before it's all torn away.

Fruits of Labor

She is a woman.
She has been told throughout the entirety of her life
Beginning at Genesis-
Conditioned-
To comply with the
Painstakingly false truth
That it's a man's world.
She is told
To be his peace,
But never speak hers.
To be his comfort,
But to never find hers.
She is undoubtedly woman,
Meticulously curated
By none other than the star dust
Like that of fellow man.
But she is spun from a different thread,
For she is the most unforgiving,
Most empowered,
Most beautiful,
Artifact of them all.

She will not be extinguished by the flaming egos
Of those who plan to put
Down such a marvelous being
In hopes to curate a certain solitude
That only originates from killing
That of a kindred spirit.

Responsible for the carriage
Of life itself;
For the sensuality many covet,
But can only witness if they ask nicely.
Or unceremoniously
Through an act of terror
And humiliation
To fortify the belief
She is less than.
But you take her for her fruit,
Because you crave the sweetness
Only she can endow.
But you forget,
Truly forget,
That while you satiated
Those otherwise carnivorous cravings
Raving her of all fruit,
She will blossom again
And she'll know she is enough.
But you,
You will always pursue what
Everyone refuses you to plague
Because
You are not craving the fruit.
No,
You are craving the fullness
You were deprived of
From the sickeningly repugnant
Lie you've been told
Your whole life.
And you,
Poor,
Pitiful thing,
Will never be able to conceptualize
That,

Contrary to popular belief,
You will never be full
From indulging upon the fruits of which
Were labored from the same breath
That same falsity was disclosed.

Color Me, Irony

I'm attracted to the feeling
Only you can evoke in me.
All the colors of the rainbow,
Shining like a kaleidoscope,
For only me to see.
The most tragic of all affairs must be
This.
For I only need you for the feeling.
All the while,
The healing begs for you
Just as much.
You cannot possibly know about this ordeal
As I ignore you to witness your appeal.

Nonsensical
And pointless.
But I'll still try,
Nonetheless.
You're unfathomable
In the sense of realism.
How ironic is it?

Essence of Quiddity

It hit me.
Like the way you realize you're walking
And you forgot why or where you're going.
It hit me.
Like the way you realize
You're blinking
And you forgot that it's something you do.
Inevitably,
Without second thoughts.
Upon this realization,
You begin to thoughtfully control it.
But eventually,
It all subsides to instinct
And you do as you were.
It hit me,
That maybe life is indeed
Not a sad story,
Nor a happy one.
In fact,
It's not much of a story at all;
It's just existence.
And who are we to think of it any other way?
Who are we to question why?
Or where?
Or in what planet or galaxy we inhabit?
Likewise,
Who are we to question
The way that man is living

When you cannot possibly fathom
Any detail of his life
From the way he projects his image?

It hit him.
Just the way it will hit you.
Maybe when you're walking,
Or blinking,
And you question-
Upon realization-
The actuality of life.
And no one can solidify the fact of it all,
It's just something we recognize
And take advantage of;
Just as we do with every breath,
Every blink,
Every stride,
Every day,
Every hour,
Every second.
And in the end,
Its that realization that will continue
To hit you.
Because the fact in question isn't why,
Or where at all.
Its not even a question.
But until acceptance is upon your lips,
Dripping like gold,
Upon your own fingertips,
Inquiry will always blister the retrospect
And conscience of a weary soul
Until it is no longer subject to neglect.

A Kiss I Will Not Miss

And I kissed misery on its
Sweet, tainted lips.
And I told him that I can no longer
Be of good company.
I'm packing my bags and leaving tomorrow
And he asked me in tears of sorrow-
One last time-
"Why now?"
As if he wasn't expecting it.
And I kissed those lips like a lazy conduit
With blank desire.
Because he was my suitor no longer.
And although misery loves company,
Leaving,
Was never something I had to ponder.

I had bought a one-way ticket
To someone I had not seen in ages.
And I missed the person
Who appeared on those tattered pages
Of a long-kept journal
From thoughts of the internal.
My longing grew stronger as I began to reach
For the person of my dreams
As misery was stuck to me like a leach.

I looked in the mirror that day,
Misery staring back at me

In eyes that resembled decay.
And I apologized for the inconvenience,
As this was never a sequence
I'd planned in my head.
Now it's time to put him to bed;
Under sheets of white satin,
Singing a lullaby in Latin,
Just to keep the mind at bay.
I'd never known
What it was like to depart
From something I had never really owned.
And what a cliché,
For me to finally know my long-lost friend
By the name of life
That very day.

Like Dissolves Like

I had found the key
But it melted in my hands.
It was made from the same
Material as my heart,
And as all things should do
When placed in hands of those who are unbeknownst,
It's destroys itself
In recoil
In order to preserve
The ways of which it operates.

The key
To my own life
Melted in my hands.
Not because I was unworthy
But because I was ignorant-
Ignorant to the bliss of life
And the bliss of loving yourself first
Before anyone or anything else.
Now it's all gone to residue.
In my palms,
Disintegrating.
All because the key to my heart
Knows.
It knows its role.
It knows its
It knows
It.

Disorder

I am begging
On my hands and knees,
Rapidly ebbing.
I need her notice what she never sees;
To look and revel,
Not gaze as if I am the devil.
I need to be caressed.
Instead I'm treated
As if I am the pest.
Please!
I am telling you,
I want to be pretty.
If only you knew-
I need not pity,
Just to have her eyes.
I am just so blue
From all these lies.
Don't let them in my dear!
I fear the end is near.
I am aching,
My heart is breaking-
Can't you feel it?
For we are so closely knit,
From the same breath we draw.
I know it an unspoken law,
But please,

Just one bite of this cheese.
I promise I'll control this craving.
Save me from this enslaving.
Please,
Save me from this disease.

A Heap of Livin'

The mantel
Just above the fireplace
Of the house that built me,
Incessantly guarded
An obscure painting of a cabin;
"A Heap of Livin'"
It captioned.
I learned to savor that painting
In all its wavering beauty.
Because,
Despite the fiery nature
And imminent death of my childhood,
It led me to accept the one affair of humanity:
Life is but a fever dream,
With the inferno of your adolescence
Mustering up a sweat upon your conscience.
The cognitive dissonance
Will begin to fray,
And you'll be enlightened about
The negligibility of our existence.
Because one day,
You'll find yourself at the crumbling steps
Of the house that built you.
And you'll remember
How you taught yourself,
At such a tender age,
The vernal silhouette of your childhood

Waving to yourself
From just outside of the front door,
That it's a heap of livin'
If you can distinguish
That you were never truly poor.

Printed in the United States
By Bookmasters